W9-BXN-196

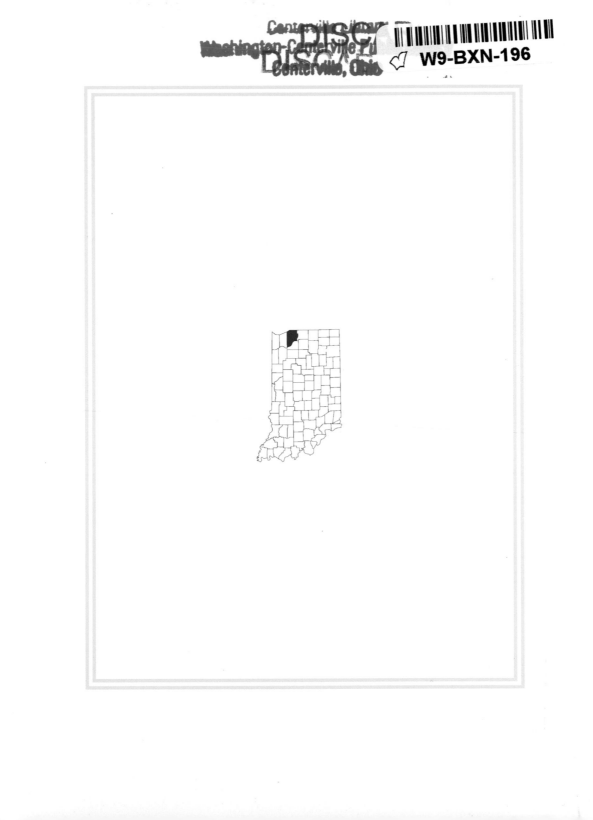

PUBLISHED BY
PRINCETON ARCHITECTURAL PRESS
37 EAST SEVENTH STREET
NEW YORK, NEW YORK 10003

FOR A FREE CATALOG OF BOOKS,
CALL 1.800.722.6657.
VISIT OUR WEB SITE AT
WWW.PAPRESS.COM.

©2006 PRINCETON ARCHITECTURAL PRESS
ALL RIGHTS RESERVED
PRINTED AND BOUND IN CHINA
09 08 07 06 5 4 3 2 1 FIRST EDITION

EDITING: JENNIFER N. THOMPSON
DESIGN: DEB WOOD

SPECIAL THANKS TO:
NETTIE ALJIAN, DOROTHY BALL,
NICOLA BEDNAREK, JANET BEHNING,
MEGAN CAREY, PENNY (YUEN PIK) CHU,
RUSSELL FERNANDEZ, JAN HAUX,
CLARE JACOBSON, JOHN KING,
MARK LAMSTER, NANCY EKLUND LATER,
LINDA LEE, KATHARINE MYERS,
LAUREN NELSON, JANE SHEINMAN,
SCOTT TENNENT, PAUL WAGNER,
JOE WESTON, AND DEB WOOD OF
PRINCETON ARCHITECTURAL PRESS
—KEVIN C. LIPPERT, PUBLISHER

LIBRARY OF CONGRESS
CATALOGING-IN-PUBLICATION DATA

LAPORTE, INDIANA / [COMPILED BY]
JASON BITNER ; FOREWORD BY ALEX
KOTLOWITZ.
   P. CM.
  ISBN-13: 978-1-56898-530-5 (HARDCOVER
: ALK. PAPER)
  ISBN-10: 1-56898-530-4 (HARDCOVER :
ALK. PAPER)
  1. LA PORTE (IND.)—BIOGRAPHY—
PORTRAITS. I. BITNER, JASON, 1974-
  F534.L3L37 2006
  977.2'91—DC22

2005016657

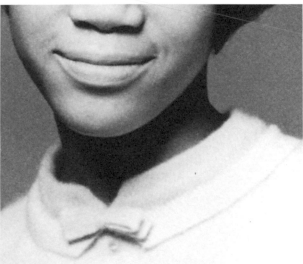

LaPorte, Indiana

Jason Bitner

Princeton Architectural Press,
New York

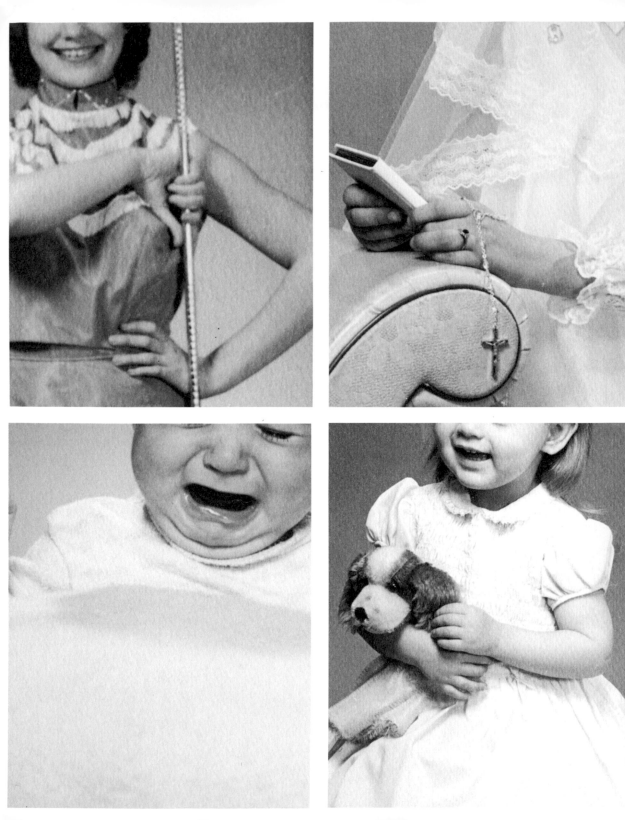

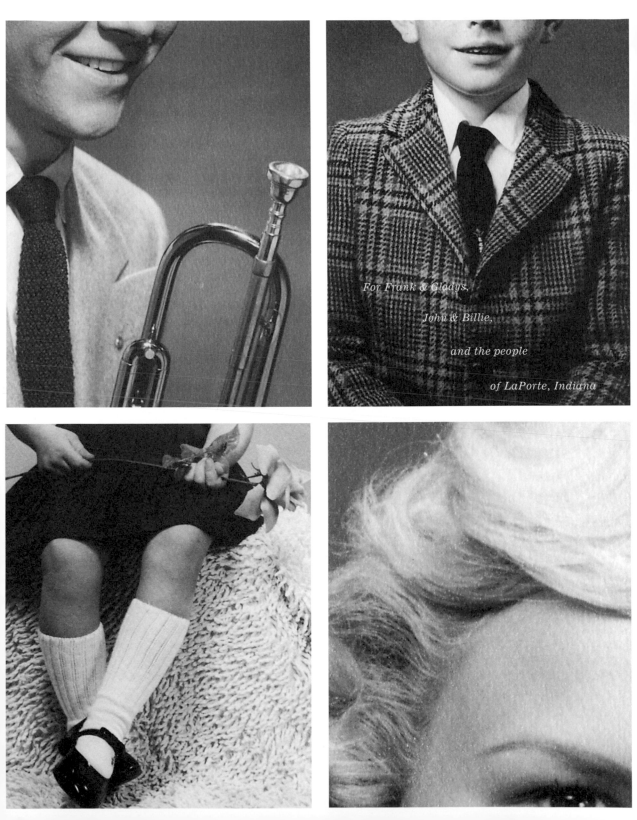

For Frank & Gladys,

John & Billie,

and the people

of LaPorte, Indiana

Foreword

by Alex Kotlowitz

Jason Bitner has made it a habit of picking up after us, walking
down the back alleys of our lives, and accumulating all that
we've thrown away or mislaid. And do we ever leave a littered
trail. Thankfully, Bitner keeps us from sweeping away our pasts.
One afternoon not long ago, over lunch at a small Midwestern
diner, Bitner stumbled onto a forgotten archive. Not the kind
you'd find at your local university library. It wasn't one that
recorded the goings and comings of the rich and powerful, but
rather one that caught the quotidian, the everyday motions
of those whom Studs Terkel calls "the et ceteras" of the world.

    It was a collection of photographs—thousands of them—of
one town's residents in the 1950s and 1960s, a time when the
country was perched on a ledge. The Great War had been won.
Factories were humming. The middle class was ballooning. And
yet right ahead of us awaited the brutal battle for civil rights,
the endless Vietnam War, and then the sputtering of American
industry. These photographs are of a time when the trail our
nation treaded was, to put it politely, messy. But what Bitner
found in these 18,000 photographs was order. People, who, for
that moment in time—when the camera's lens shuttered—
seemed impervious to the upheaval around them. A pigtailed
girl dreamily peering skyward. A couple holding hands, looking
lovingly at each other (the man with daringly long sideburns).
A sailor in uniform. An older married couple. A woman clutching
a rose. They are admittedly brief moments, and ones in which
people have purposefully posed for the camera. It's how these
people of LaPorte, Indiana wanted to be remembered. Smiling.
Caring. (There's an especially moving picture of one elderly man
straightening a friend's tie). Loving. Pensive. Serious. Often in
their finest clothes. Their hair combed just right. Their expres-
sions just as they want.

The faces in this book are distinctly middle American. Open. Unassuming. Sturdy. This is the heartland after all, a land of dreamers and pragmatists, a grounded people struggling to reconcile promise with reality. And the power of these photographs lies not in their art or their candor, but rather in their self-consciousness. They're remarkable for what they say about our desire to be seen in a certain light: twirling a baton, sniffing a rose, deep in thought, laughing, flirtatious. It's as if the photographer said to them: let me see you as you see yourself.

But we, of course, know better. It's the vagaries of life. To look at these photographs is to look at a collection of short stories, or at least the stories' opening pages. They bring to mind Sherwood Anderson's *Winesburg, Ohio* in which lives unfurled and unraveled in a manner that was anything but tidy. You look at these photographs and begin to imagine the stories behind them. The twists and turns each of them took in the months and years afterwards. You wonder whatever came of the young girl's dreams. Or whether the handholding couple kept their love intact. Or if the sailor was sent to Vietnam, and if so, whether he made it back. What Bitner found here are not complete stories, but rather a moment in these journeys. A snapshot in the truest sense of the word. These photographs provide an opening into these lives, into this town, into the heart of our nation.

What Jason Bitner has assembled here is nothing short of astonishing. And it's unsettling to think that had he not gone to this diner and lingered over his cinnamon rolls, these photographs, these stories might have been discarded or simply lost. Bitner is the equivalent of a nearsighted archeologist. He looks for clues to our lives. Only his time is not measured by eons, but rather in years and decades. And what he finds are hints to what has transpired and what is about to unfold. Thumb through these pages, linger over these photographs, examine the faces, and you will be transported, to a place and to a time, when America wrestled with its very identity, when we struggled with how we wanted to be perceived.

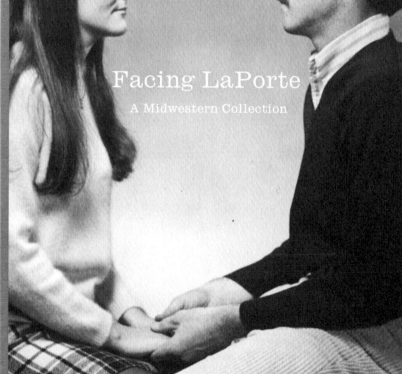

Facing LaPorte

A Midwestern Collection

A Frank C. Pease Portrait

The highway from my home in Chicago to LaPorte, Indiana hugs the southeastern edge of Lake Michigan. Heading away from Chicago's landmark skyscrapers, you soon pass the rundown high-rises of the South Side, bypass the smokestacks and casinos of Hammond and Gary, Indiana, and exit near the scenic Michigan City, Indiana.

The roads become smaller and more affected by the quiet rolls of pastureland and the out-of-place vineyard. You'll pass a small airport, some garage sales and cigarette stores, and a few horses. You'll cross the train tracks, which supplied this former vacation destination with visitors from Chicago. And before long, Lake Michigan and her surrounding sandy dunes will be left in the rearview mirror, and a smallish Midwestern town will appear near the edge of South Pine Lake.

*

A few years back, I got wind of the LaPorte County Fair and its legendary demolition derby. Legendary like your ears will ring until Monday and you might get lucky and see a super-sized man booty-dancing on the roof of his broke-down station wagon. Not to mention this very fair has brought people together each year since 1836—before radio, before my grandparents were born, and even before the California Gold Rush. With this in mind, a friend and I drove out toward the fairgrounds early on a beautiful Saturday morning to guarantee some tickets for the evening's show.

*

When heading to LaPorte, you use the monstrous overpass (built to ensure that eighteen wheelers would have an efficient in-and-out of the city), and drive by the monumental courthouse designed by Chicago's acclaimed city planner, Daniel Burnham, in 1894. If you stop by the local historical society situated behind the courthouse, you might learn about the Kingsbury Ordnance Plant, the local munitions factory, which produced a huge number of shells for World War II. You might come across early farming equipment and the re-creation of a settler's parlor room, and you might learn that LaPorte, "the door," was so named because its prairie land allowed an easy passage to the new frontier, the West.

*

Traveling into town on the sleepy thoroughfare, we decided to stop for a quick bite at B & J's American Café, a classic old diner complete with an enormous counter, local gossip and friendly teens taking orders. Checking the menu, I noticed the cinnamon roll requires an extra fifteen minutes, and if a menu item asks for additional time, it must be a specialty. We ordered three and spent a few minutes watching people come and go.

As we sipped coffee at the counter and reviewed the *LaPorte Herald-Argus*, I noticed a couple of beautiful 5" x 7" black and white photos taped to the pie case. The paper was slightly yellowed and showing a few signs of wear, but these amazing portraits were from an entirely different era.

*

A couple years back, I helped create a show-and-tell project of discovered notes and photographs called *Found Magazine*. People from around the world sent us their discoveries, from lost and forgotten love letters to extensive and exhausting lists, from Polaroids to classroom notes—anything that gives a peek into another person's life.

Sometimes a find comes as a loaded twenty-word missive and other times we'll receive an entire journal detailing an extended family's history. Our intention is to see how people's worlds are often very different in specifics—race and class and ability to spell—but also how we share similar emotions and difficulties and joys. Oftentimes all we know is our own world, and we can easily forget about lives that don't directly impact our own.

After tens of thousands of submissions, I've grown accustomed to receiving these wonderful and unexpected finds in my mailbox, and every once in a while there's a treasure in the alley behind my apartment. As the project brings dozens of to-do lists, missives from angry neighbors, and break-up notes to us each week, I've learned where to look for the prized keepers.

Nothing I've seen since the project began, however, could match the scale of what I was about to happen upon in the diner.

*

I asked the waitress about the photos and she pointed toward a door leading to an unused dining area. The near side of the room was reserved for rolling silverware into paper napkins, while the back of the room housed two large metal shelving units holding twenty-two cardboard boxes. These boxes were stuffed with stacks and stacks of photos, all with remarkably similar characteristics. Initially, I guessed we were looking at two to three thousand photos, though I'd later hand count nearly eighteen thousand of these beauties.

"Find a family member! Photos $.50 each—or—$5.00 for a packet," stated a small sign to the right of the shelves. Before us stood a nearly complete archive documenting the townspeople of mid-century LaPorte for sale—cheap!—in a quiet room of a local eatery. We rifled through an entire town's population, as if it were a card catalog, a huge visual archive of Midwestern faces that were being unloaded two-for-a-dollar.

*

Diner owner John Pappas grew up in the building; he and his wife Billie passed along the details.

Back in the 1950s and 60s, the building's second floor was home to Muralcraft Studios. Frank and Gladys Pease made their living by crafting kid's photos, anniversary shots, senior portraits, engagement announcement pictures, and portraits for any event that called for a formal sitting. Frank photographed, while Gladys took care of the administrative end of the business and helped clients look their best for this special occasion.

A typical client would climb a long set of stairs, enter a small waiting area and be greeted by Gladys. After taking their coats, she would lead the subjects to either the men's or women's dressing room, and sit them before a mirror. Makeup might be applied, hair combed, ties adjusted, teeth checked for spinach. When everything looked satisfactory, they would head down a short hallway to greet Frank.

The back half of the space housed the studio, darkroom, and a storage area for props and the especially large lighting equipment. Pease shot with a medium-format camera (a few of the negatives still exist) and once he established his technique, he never wavered from the look; sitters' hair and clothing styles changed over time, though the art direction never budged. This was not ego-driven work—Pease simply offered himself as a skilled photographer for hire and put clients' needs before his own. Clearly he viewed his photography as a trade or a craft instead of an art form.

The photos that follow were never intended as final prints; rather these are proofs that were shipped to clients so they could determine which shot was most becoming, would look best on the mantle, or would be the most flattering to send to loved ones across the country. As clients were offered black and white or hand-colored final images, handwritten notes detailing the color of eyes, hair, and clothing mark the backs of these proofs to ensure eyes weren't mistakenly tinted blue rather than hazel.

After running Muralcraft for decades, Frank Pease passed away in the early 1970s. Prior to his death, Pease kindly donated his photo equipment to the local high

LAPORTE STATISTICS

- - - - - - - - - - - - - -

Definition of LaPorte means "the door" in French. It was called this by the French fur traders who came here in the 1600s. They found a natural opening in the forests which lead to the prairies beyond, so they called this opening LaPorte.

- - - - - - - - - - - - - -

County Seat
LaPorte

Founded
1832

Size
608 square miles

Elevation
700 to 850 feet on average
The highest point in LaPorte County is 957 feet above sea level. It is located on a knoll east of Lambs Chapel in Galena Township, about 6.5 miles north of the city of LaPorte.
　　The lowest point in the county is 581 feet above sea level. It is located on the shore of Lake Michigan.

Time Zone
Central Standard Time, changing to Central Daylight Saving Time from the first Sunday in April to the last Sunday in October.

Climate
Lake Michigan has a strong influence on the climate of LaPorte County. Temperatures in January range from a low of 15 degrees to a high of 32 degrees. Temperatures in July range from a low of 61 degrees to a high of 85 degrees. The average annual precipitation is 40 to 45 inches, which is high for this part of the state. The average annual snowfall accumulations are the state's highest, from 45 to 75 inches!

Location
Located west of South Bend, on the Michigan border, with its northwestern boundaries on the shores of Lake Michigan. LaPorte County is intersected by Interstate Highways 80, 90, 94, and US Highway 30.

Population
The 2000 census listed 110,106 residents which increased by 2.8% from 1990

Nickname
The Hoosier State

State Bird
Cardinal

State Flower
Peony

State Song
"On the Banks of the Wabash, Far Away"

State Tree
Tulip tree

clockwise from top left LaPorte Courthouse;
residential street; 607 Lincolnway (second
floor housed Muralcraft Studios, with
B & J's American Café on the ground floor);
and the prairie on the outskirts of LaPorte

school (and it's likely that some of the younger subjects honed their darkroom skills on the very enlarger of their first portrait) and the proofs were all left in the studio. These photos sat in storage for over twenty years, until Billie and John opened their restaurant in the early nineties. For the past decade, these photos have been quietly sitting for sale in their back room, along with a few remainders of the lighting setup, while the Muralcraft studio has been renovated into a spacious apartment.

*

So we hunkered down on the floor, picked up a few stacks of photos and were instantly transfixed. Flipping through the pictures, we discovered an enormous visual survey of the Midwest a generation back. These faces staring back conjured family members, close friends, distant acquaintances—even Hollywood glamour shots. The collection reads like an incredibly beautiful census, with expertly lit faces replacing biographical data. By carrying on with his commercial photo business practice, Pease unwittingly created an enormous and compelling historical document. He became an accidental historian.

We ordered our second meal and kept digging. Halfway through the first box, I'd already committed to somehow taking in each of the eighteen thousand photos. It's addicting, and overwhelming, and you don't just come across something this incredible and soon forget about it. Three boxes into the process, I decided to spend a week straight in the back room of B & J's, sipping coffee, reading the local paper, and selecting a couple hundred of my favorites to share.

I discovered it's real easy to become image-fatigued when handling hundreds of photos each day; this kind of repetition leads to excitement for oddballs and more peculiar photos. I tried to steer clear of this kind of sensationalism when choosing photos for this book. The pictures that follow

Muralcraft Studio
605½ LINCOLN WAY
LA PORTE, INDIANA

clockwise from top left Frank and Gladys Pease;
a Muralcraft photograph envelope; B & J's
back room with the Pease collection; the
Pease archive; Gladys in the dressing room

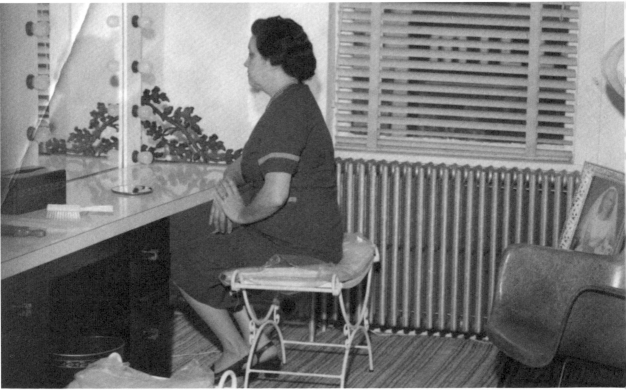

are organized and ordered, though the themes may not always be obvious.

*

Pease became a stenographer of LaPorte. He surely didn't intend on a life as a cultural secretary, but his career and his work have gained an importance beyond that of each individual image. For a single anniversary photo holds a little historical value, but a collection this vast, spanning over a generation will certainly hold greater cultural value.

And that the collection should come from LaPorte— the door, the entryway—well, the metaphor is almost embarrassingly obvious. Come take a peek at the Midwest in the 1950s and 60s . . .

Acknowledgments

BIG AND HEARTFELT THANKS GO TO

JOHN AND BILLIE PAPPAS AT B&J'S AMERICAN CAFÉ,

POLLY NOONAN AND DAN RYBICKY,

ED AND EVE NOONAN AND EVERYONE AT TRYON FARM,

JENNIFER THOMPSON,

ALISSA SHIPP,

JULIE SHAPIRO,

AND JENNIFER TROYER.

THIS BOOK WOULDN'T BE POSSIBLE WITHOUT YOUR HELP.

THANKS ALSO TO

XAN ARANDA, LESLIE BAUM, JOHN AND DANIELA BITNER,

LESLIE BROWN, MARCO CALLEGARI, NANCY FORD, EMILY GABRIAN,

NICOLE KALKBRENNER, JUD LAGHI, THE LAPORTE HERALD-ARGUS,

HOLLY MATTHEWS, HARRIET MENOCAL, BOB MERLIS,

KELLY MILLER, ELIZABETH QUINLAN, CAROL ROSS,

FERN EDDY SCHULTZ, JOSHUA WOLF SHENK,

KAY AND JAY STRAYER, AND AARON WICKENDEN.

THANK YOU ALL SO MUCH.

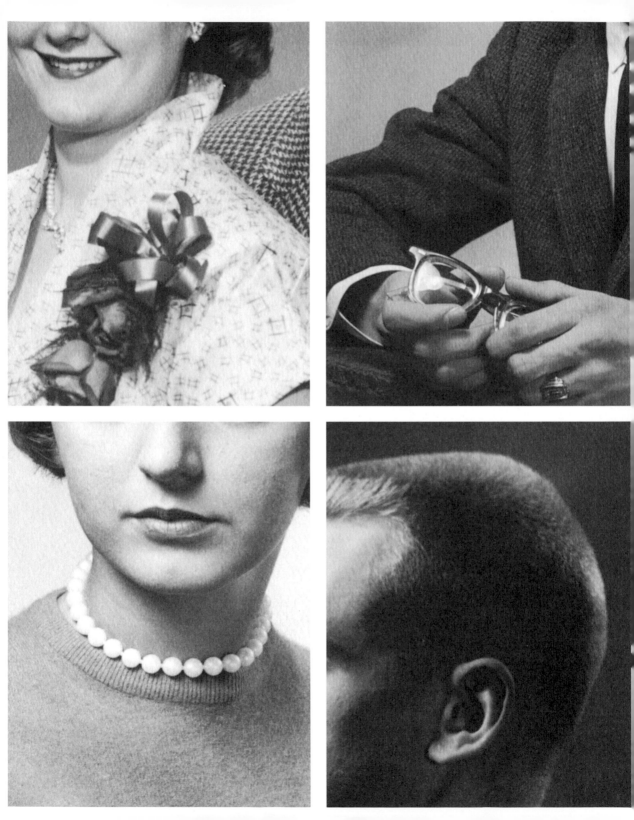

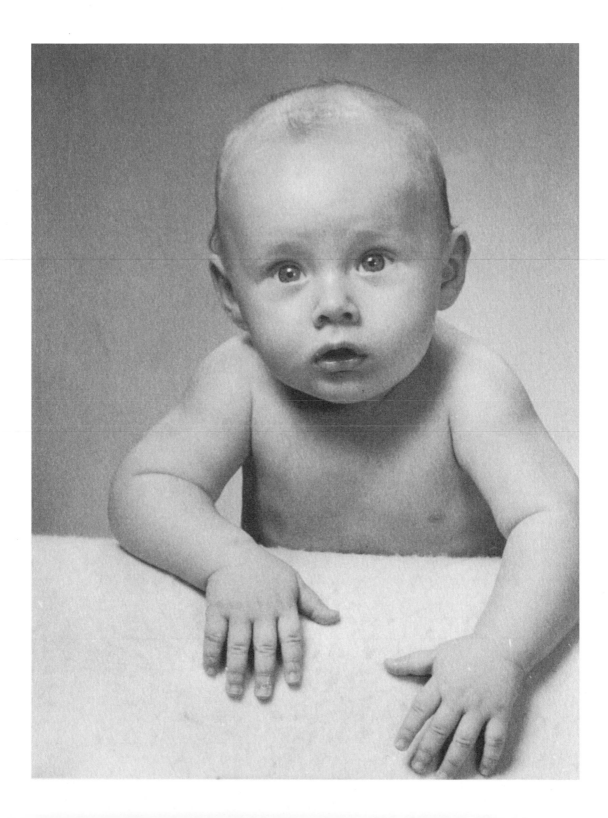

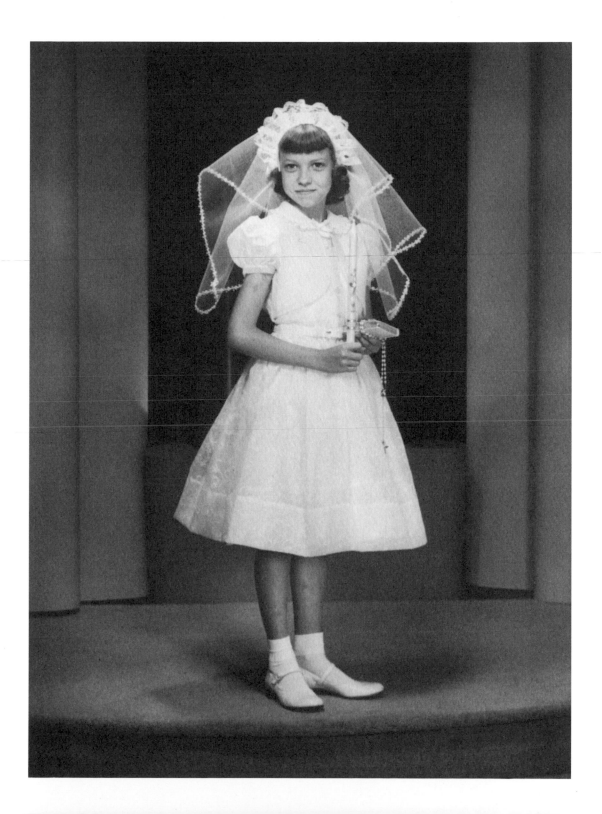

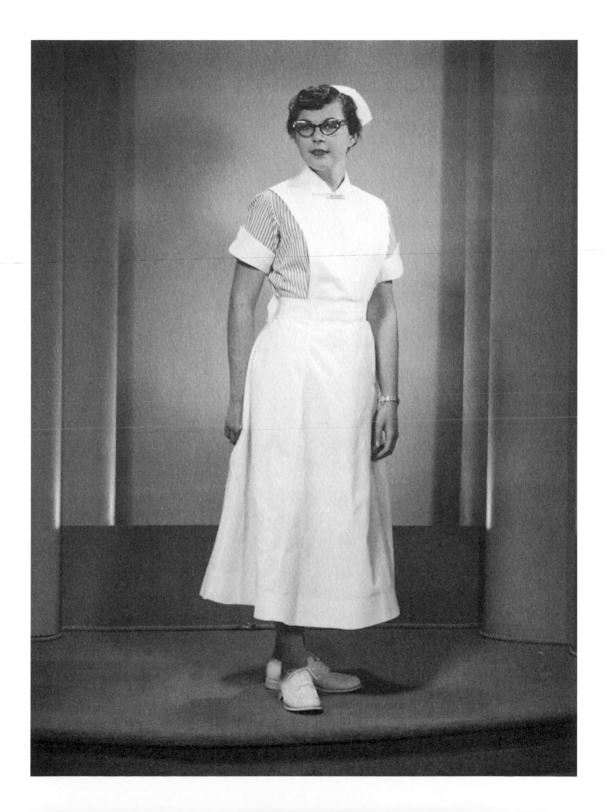

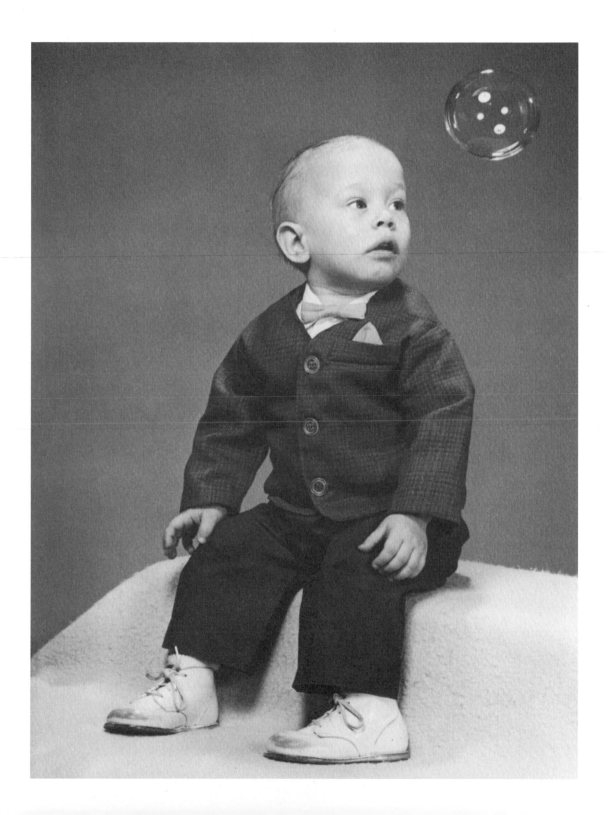

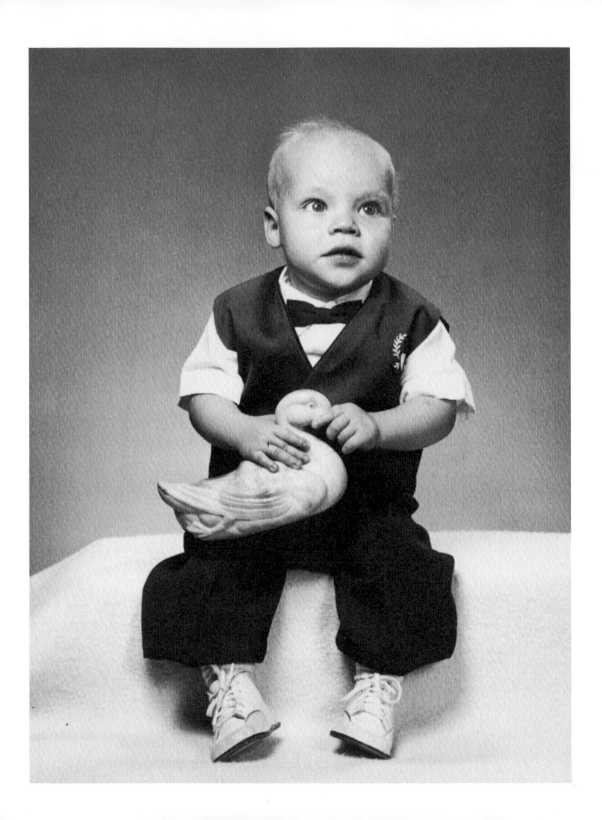

album color

- - - - - - - - - - - - - - -

HAIR
blonde

EYES
blue

SUIT
red vest

blue pants

tie blue

blue piping on vest

white + blue design

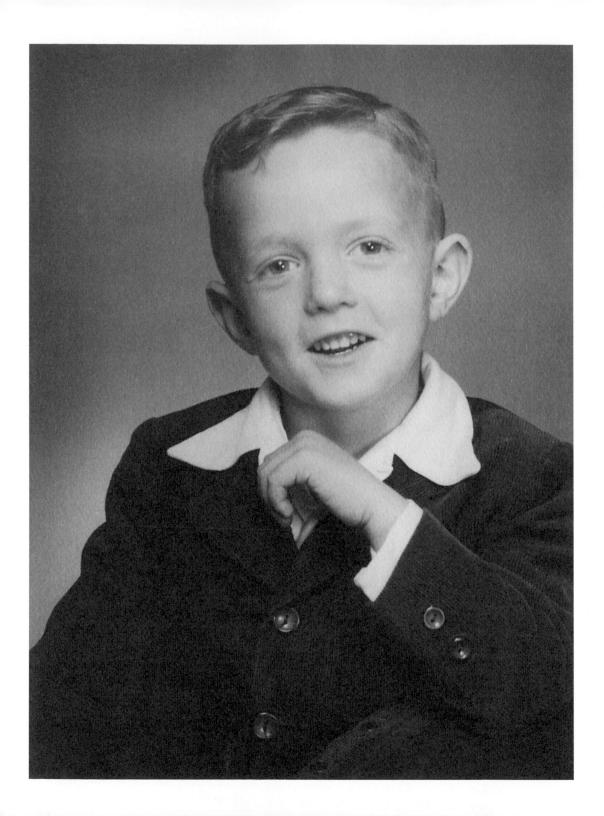

[*handwritten on back*]

1 8x10 color

B.R. blankard frame

- - - - - - - - - - - - - -

HAIR

v dk. brown

EYES

brown

DRESS

pwd blue

GLASSES

dk rose with gold

EARRINGS AND NECKLACE

rhinestone

RING

gold set. diamonds

WATCH

gold

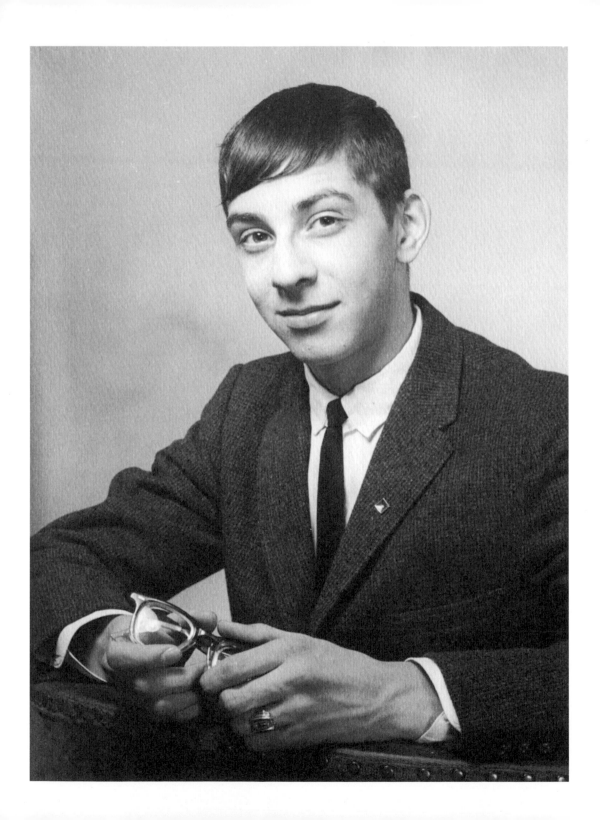

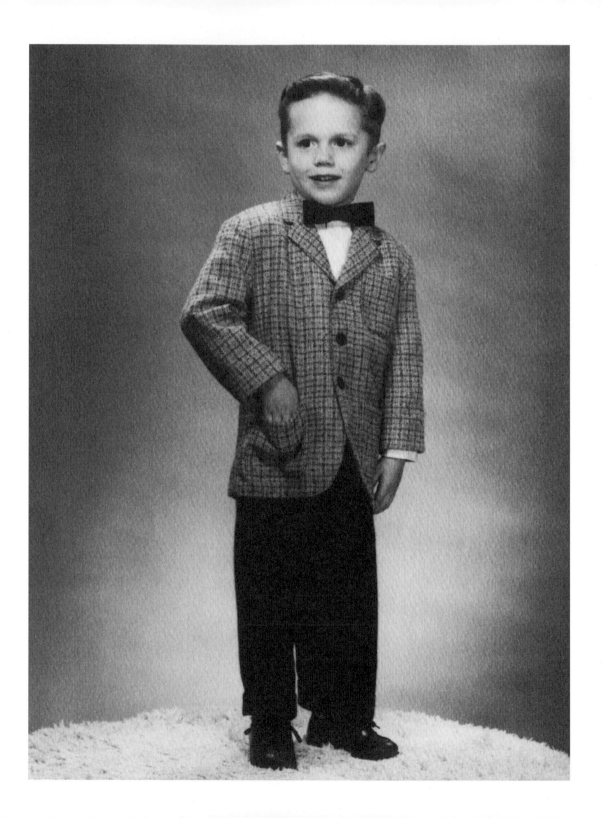

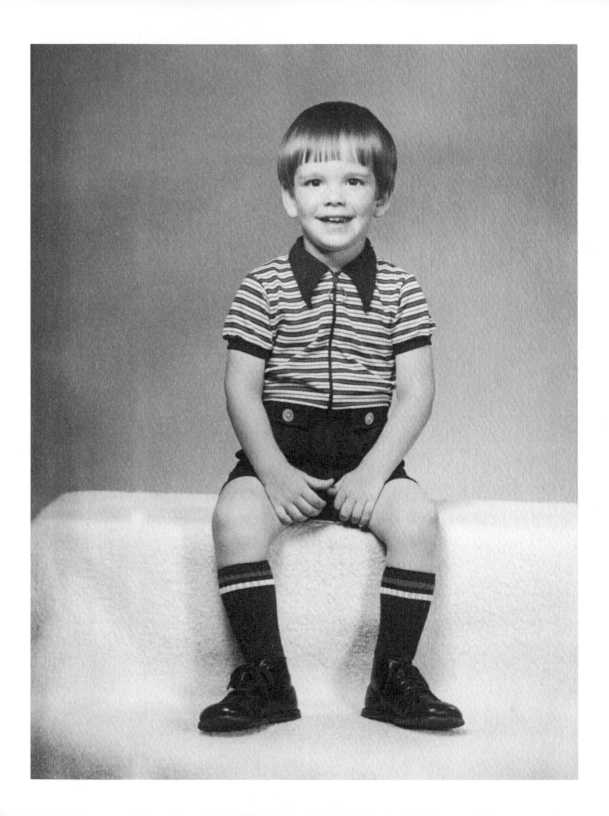

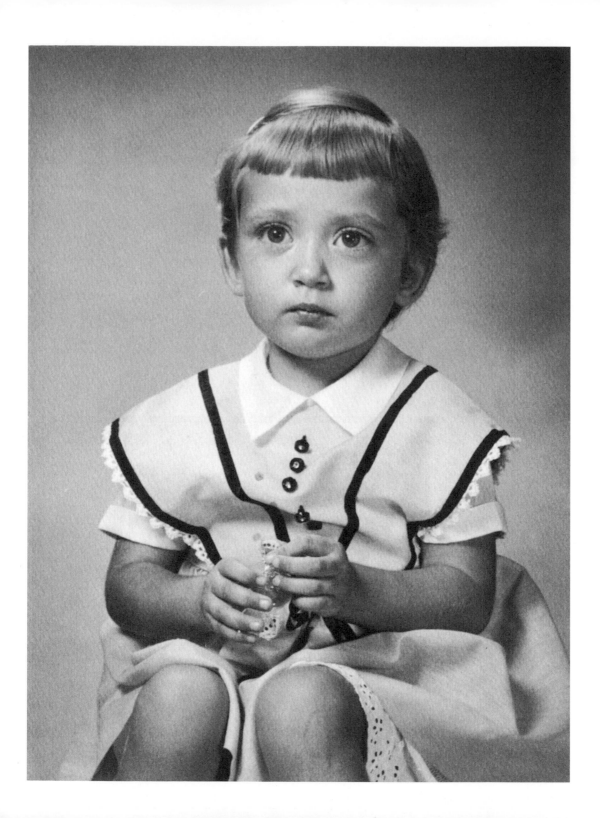

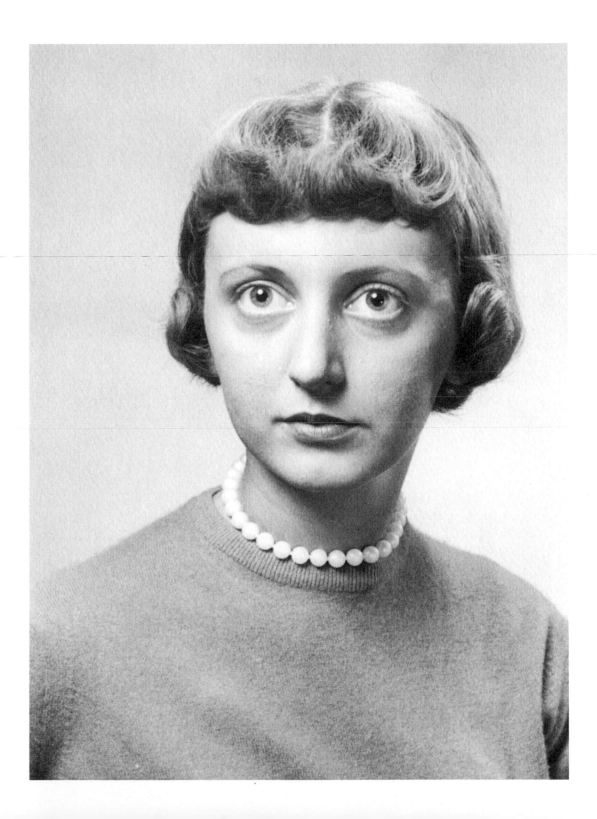

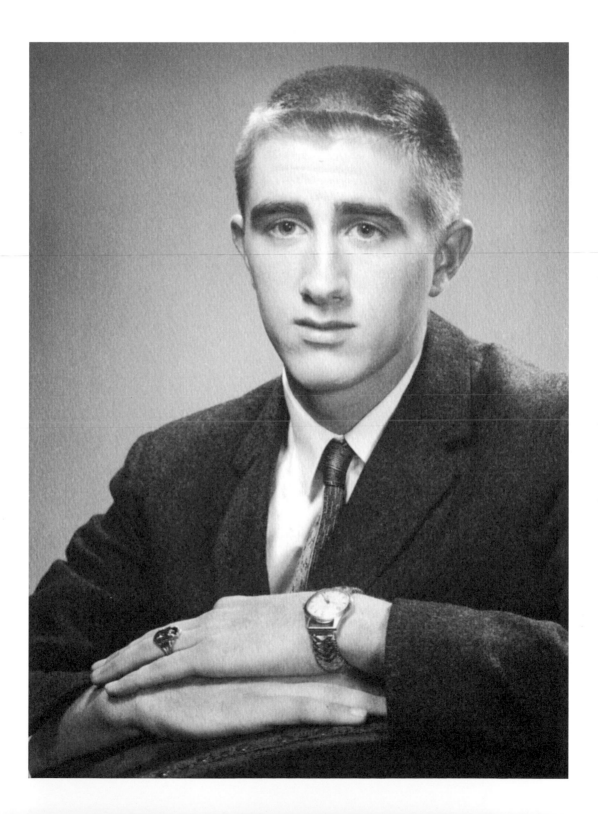

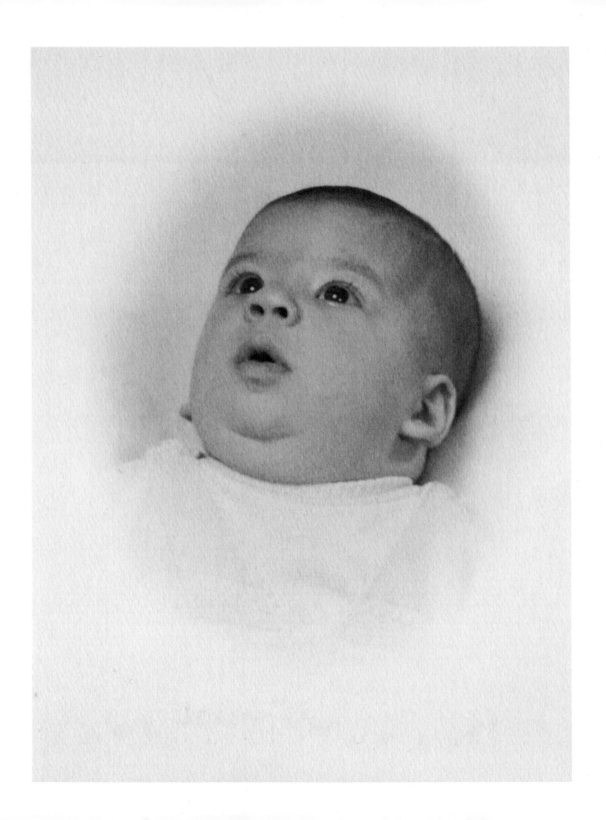

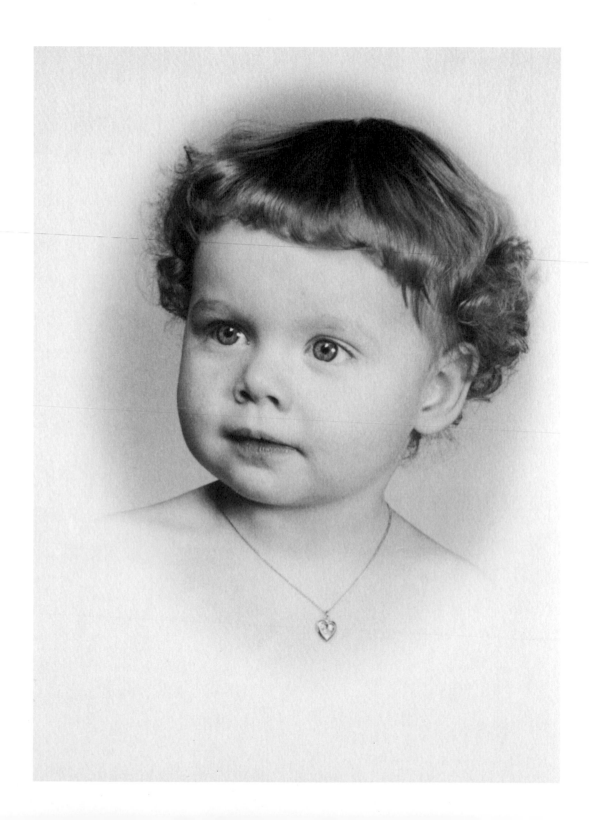

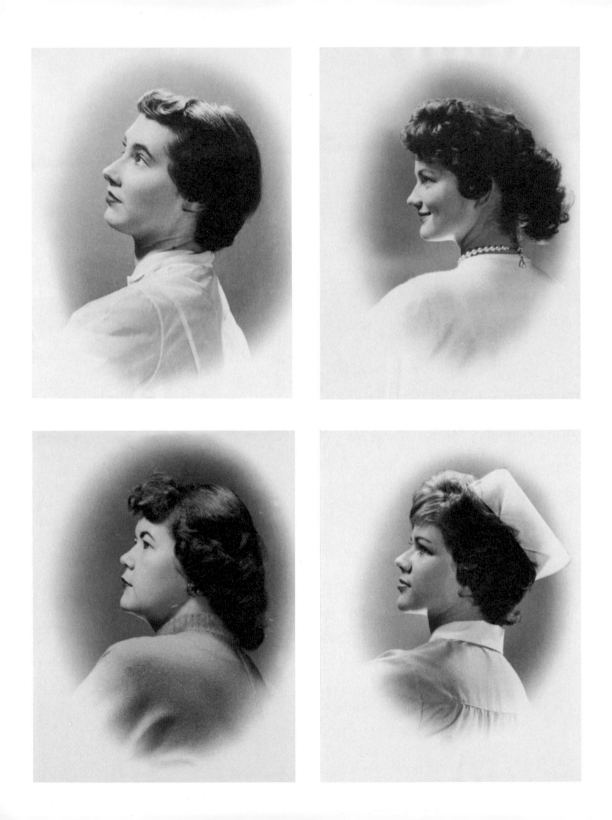

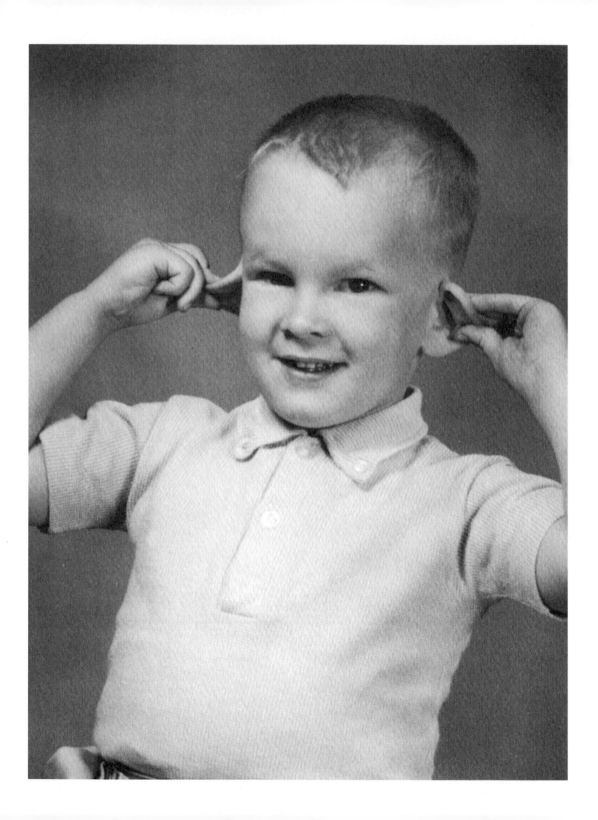

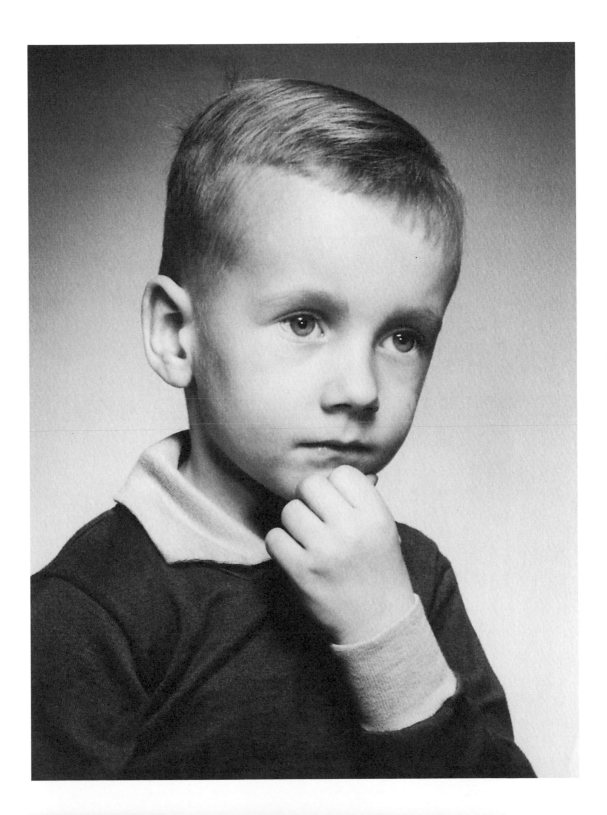

50 reprints

1   8 x 10 color.

- - - - - - - - - - - - - - -

HAIR
blonde

EYES
blue

LIPS
pink

SWEATER
aqua

NECKLACE
pearls

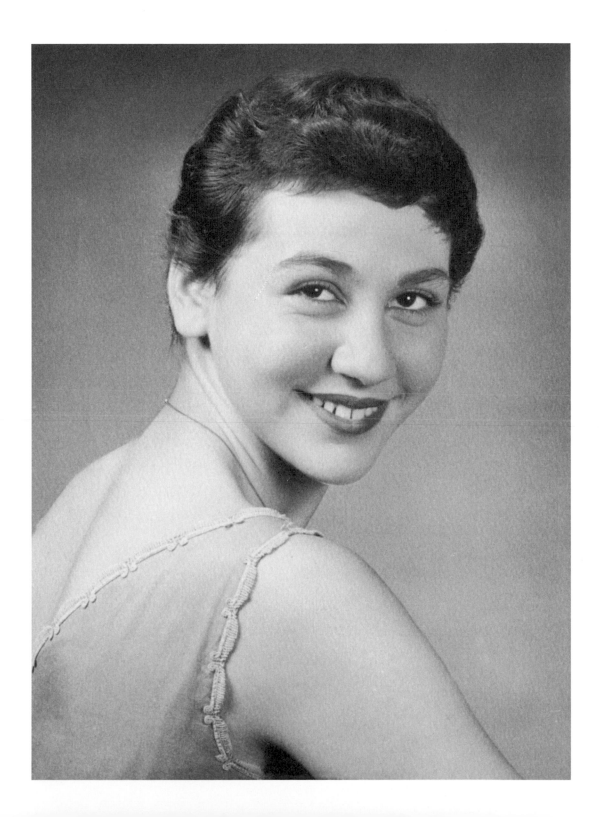

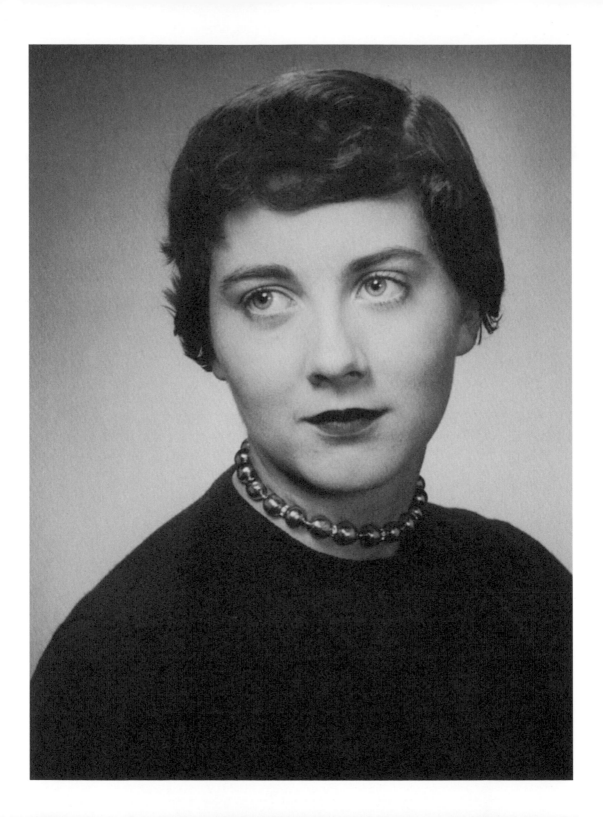

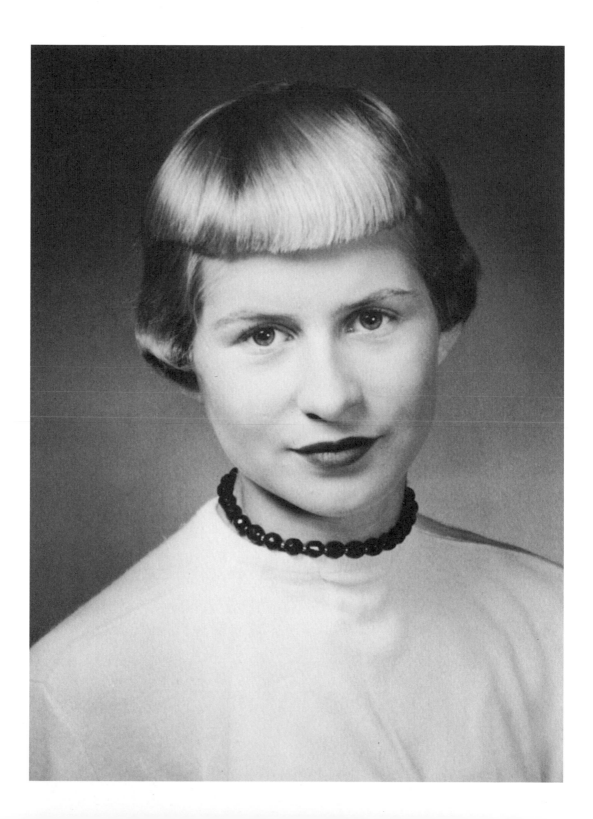

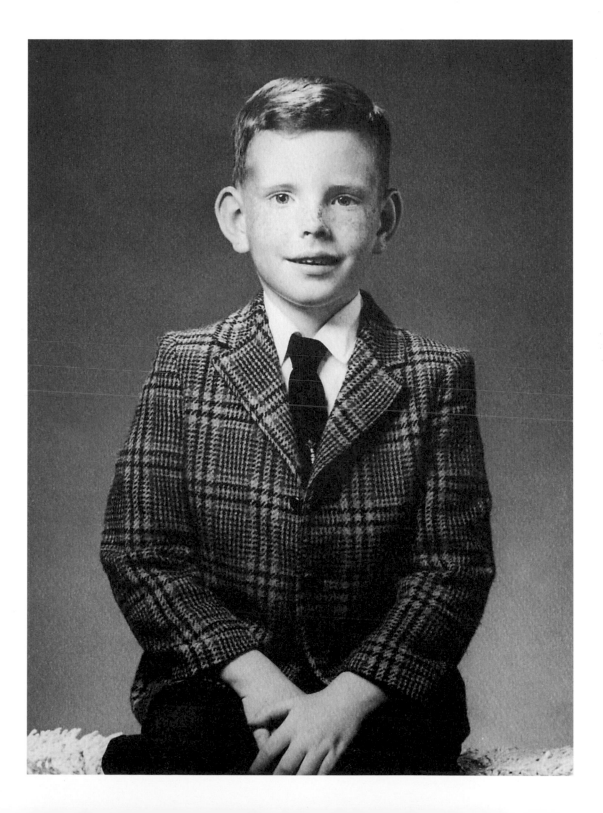

[*handwritten on back*]

album color.

- - - - - - - - - - - - - - -

HAIR
blonde

EYES
blue

HAT
red

SHIRT
white
red + blue trim
red + blue reacquets
red ball

SHOES
blue

SOX
white-red stripe

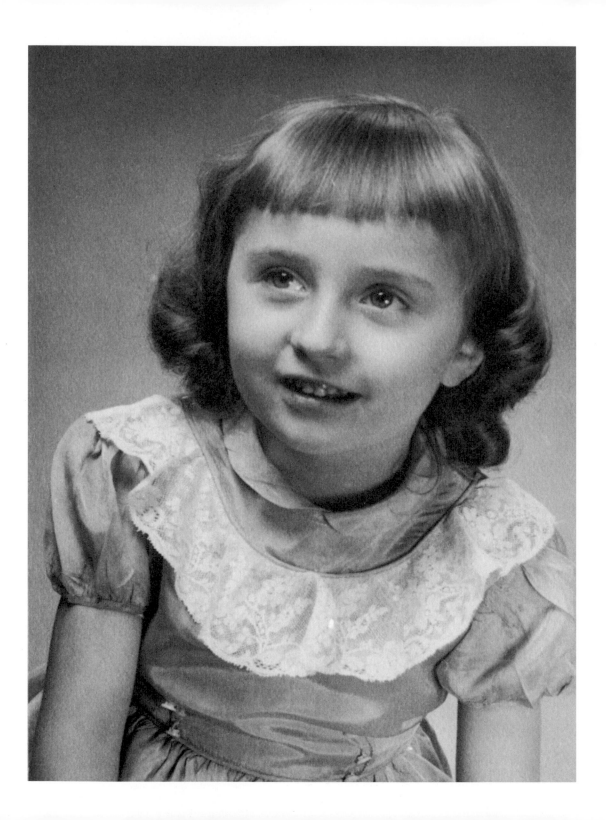

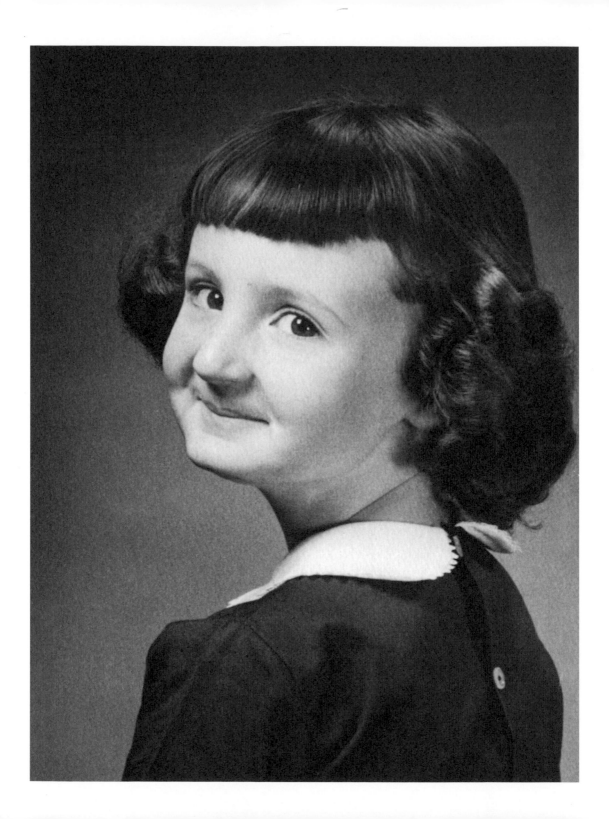

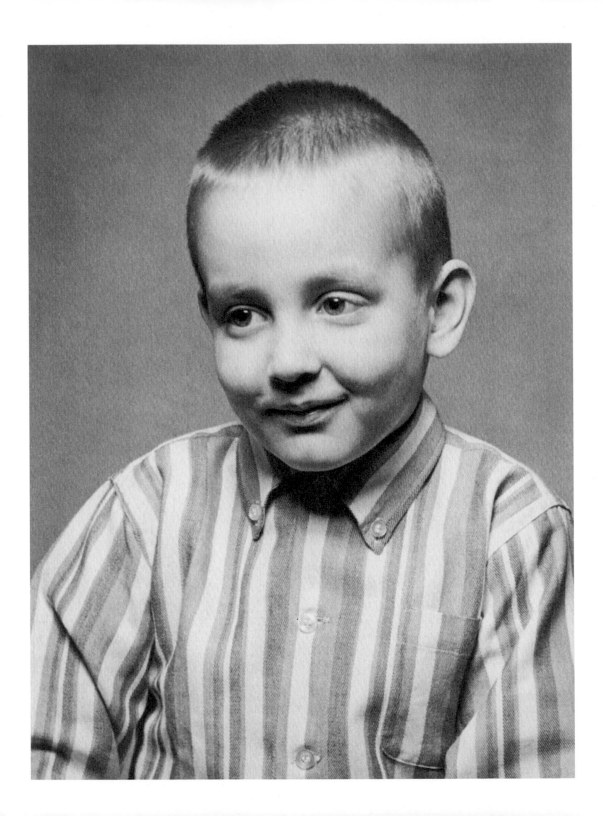

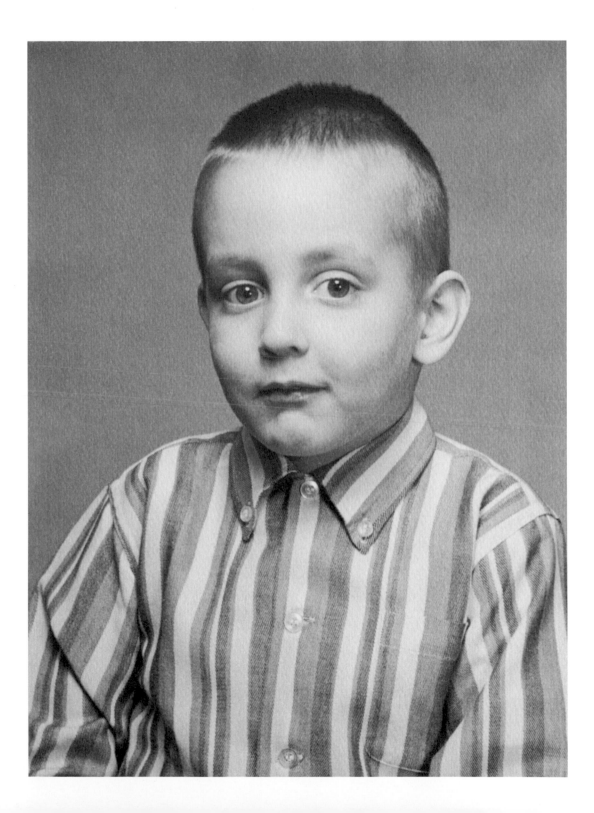

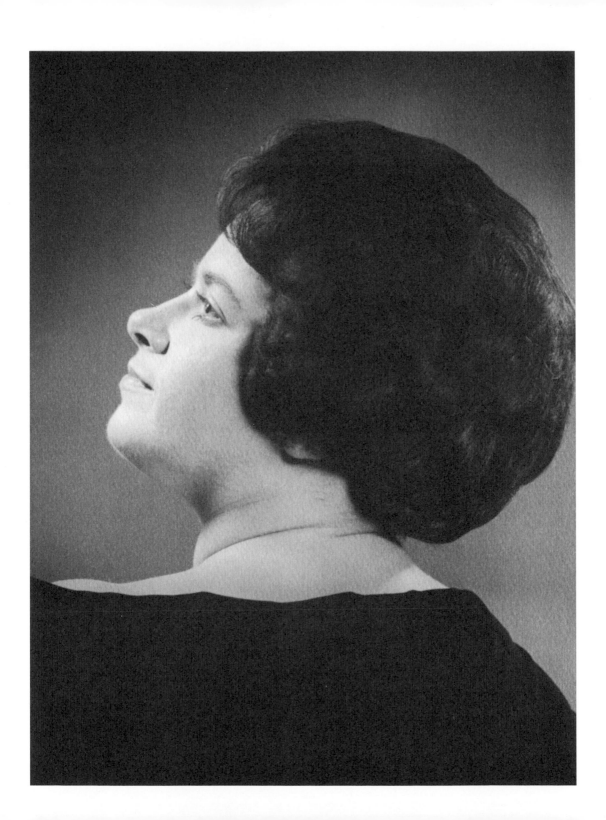

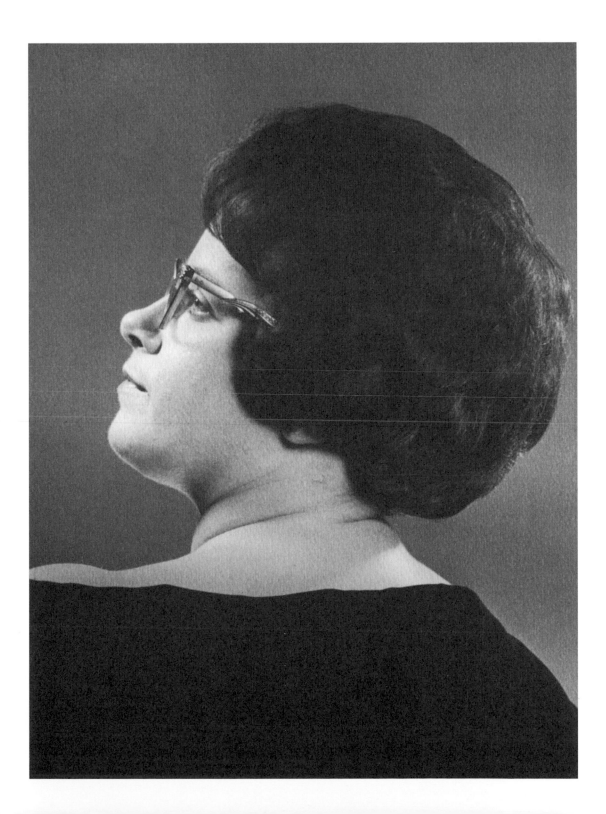

"...and if I am elected..."

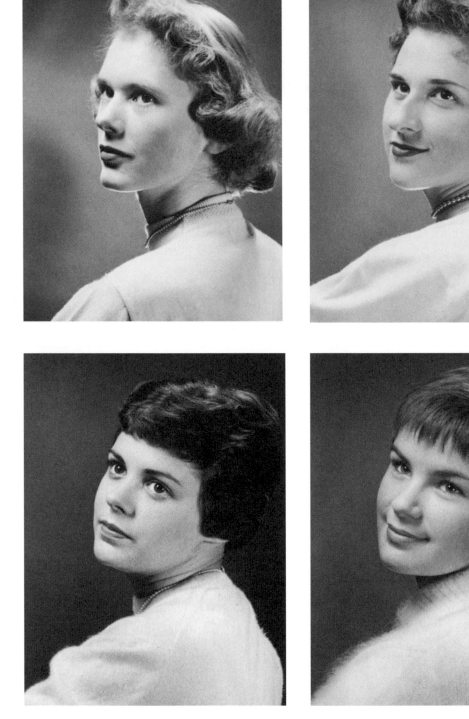

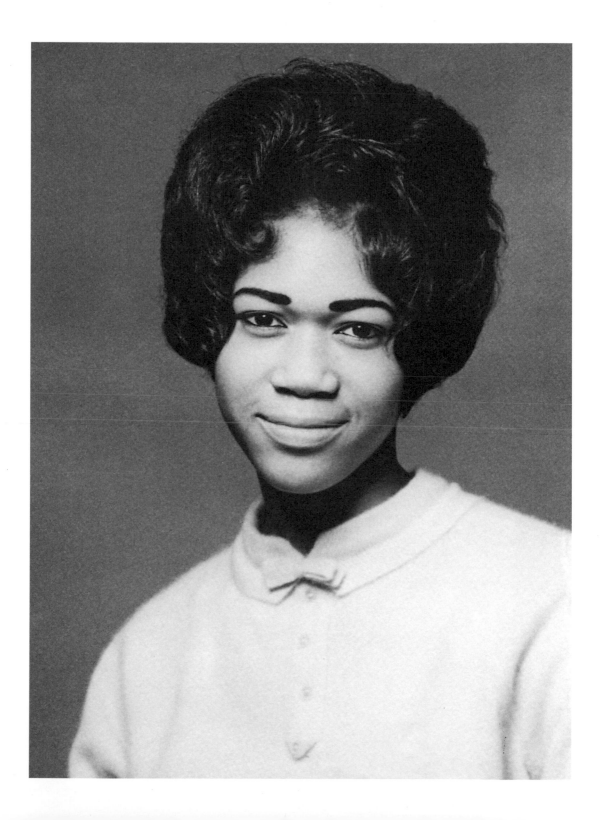

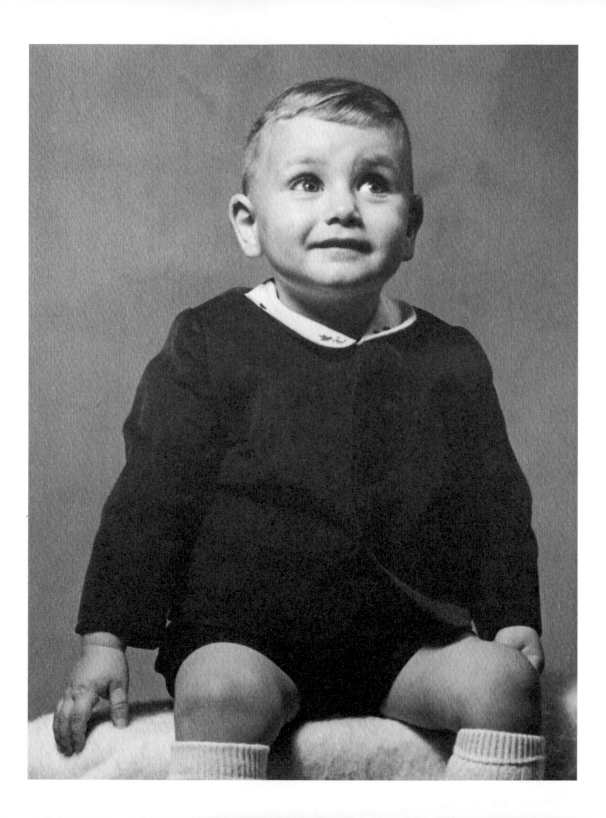

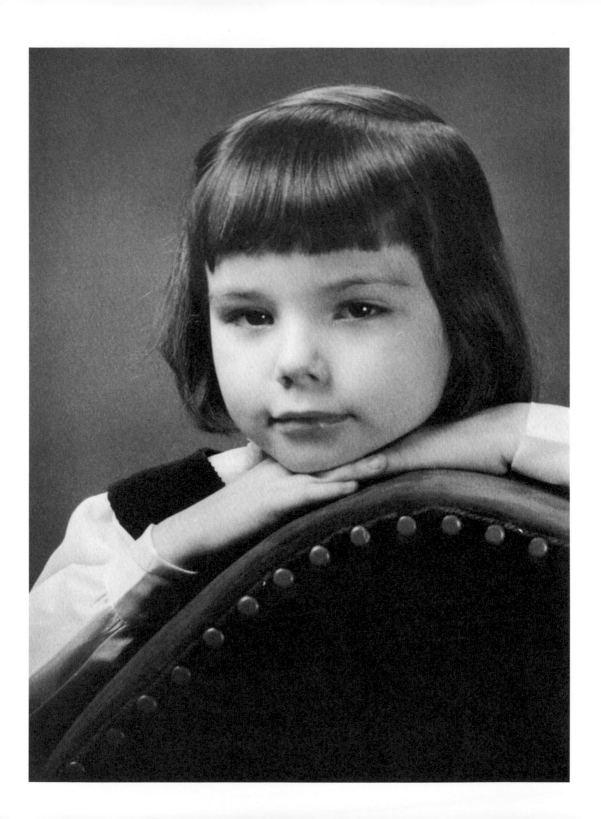

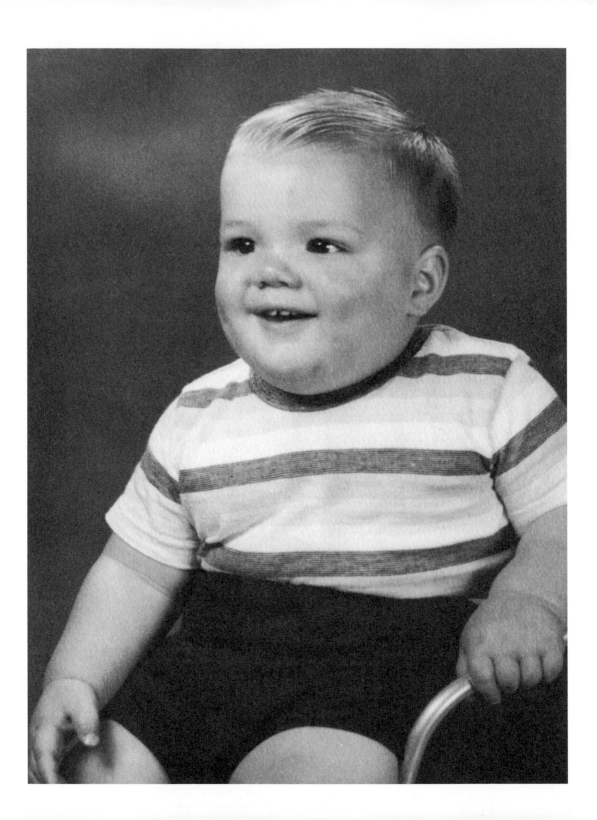

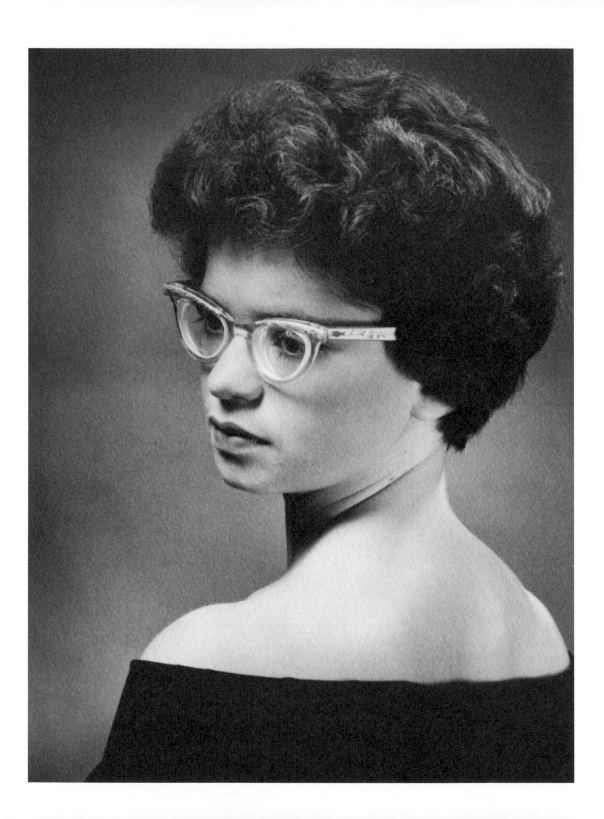

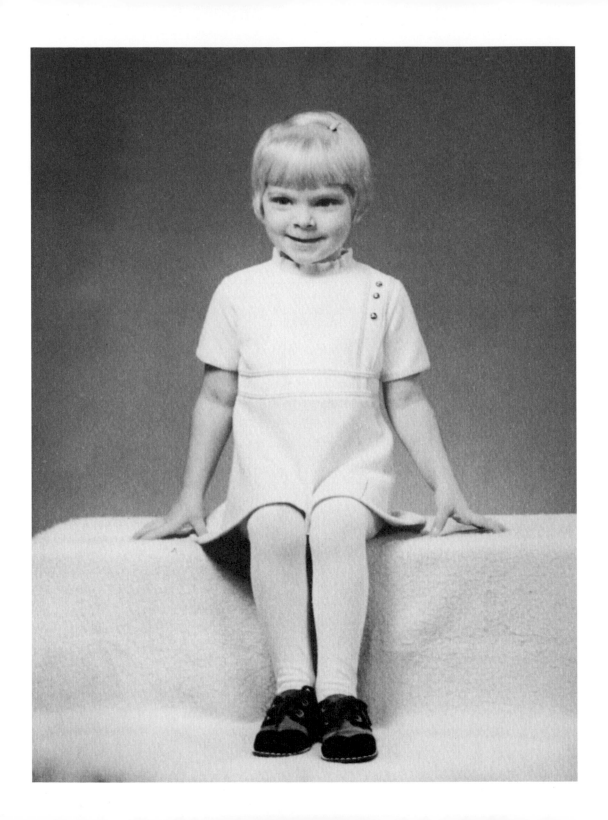

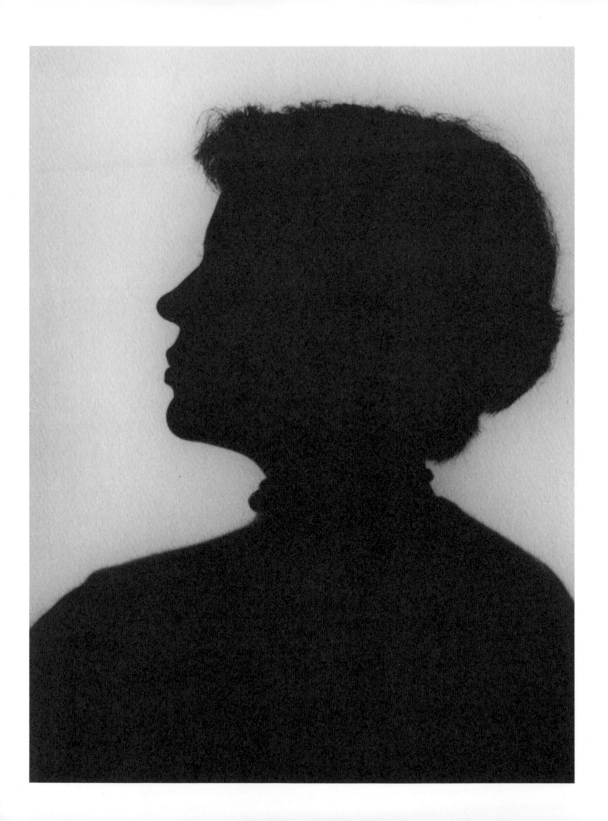

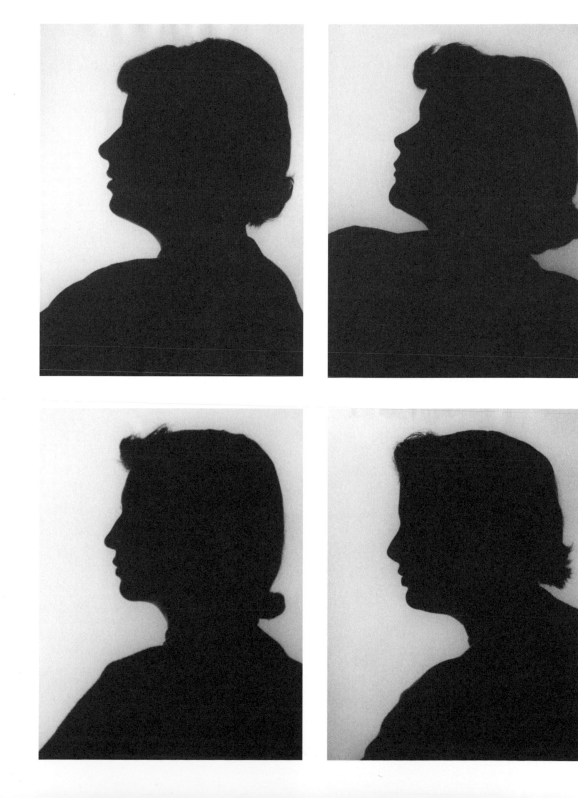

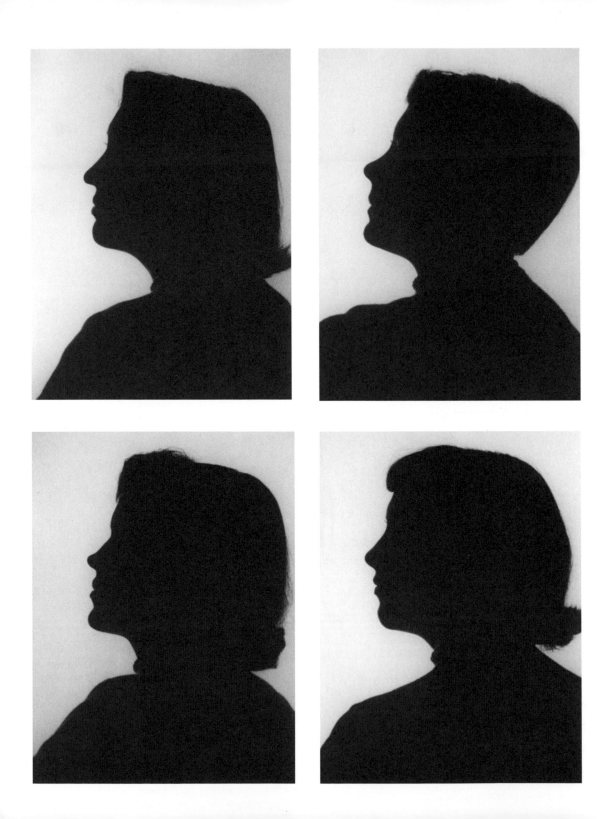

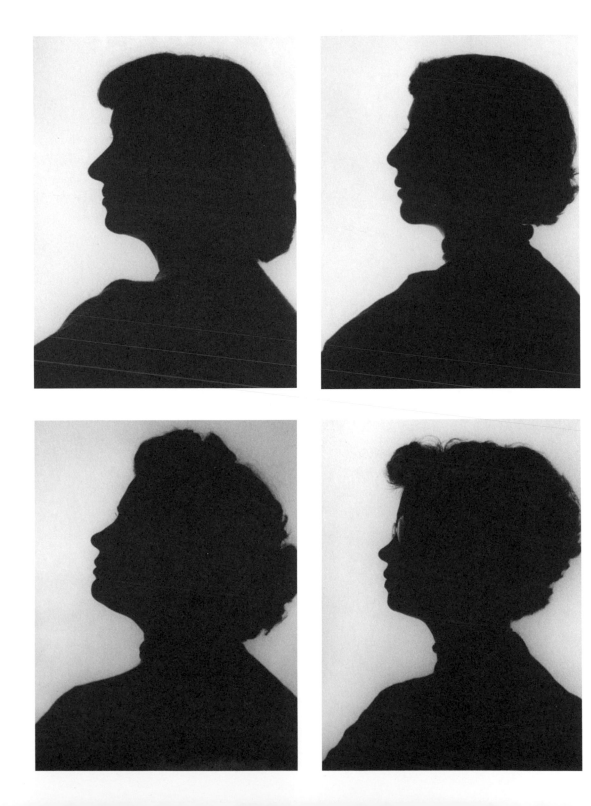

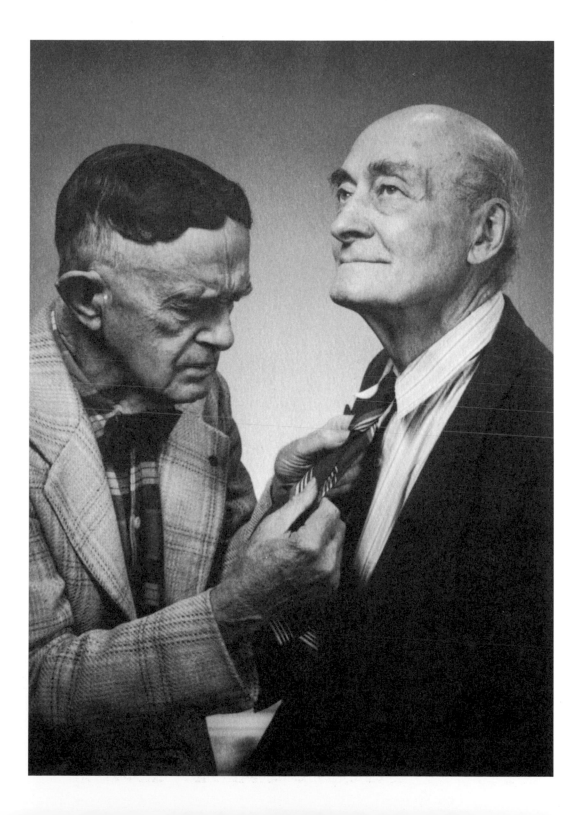